TO:

Linda

FROM:

Linda

All I Really Need to Know I Learned in Kindergarten

THE ESSAY THAT BECAME A CLASSIC

with a Special Commentary by

Robert Fulghum

VILLARD BOOKS · NEW YORK · 1991

Copyright © 1986, 1990 by Robert Fulghum
Portrait © 1990 by Karen Lewis

All rights reserved under International and Pan-American
Copyright Conventions. Published in the United States by
Villard Books, a division of Random House, Inc.,
New York, and simultaneously in Canada by Random House
of Canada Limited, Toronto.
The essay "All I Really Need to Know I Learned
in Kindergarten" originally appeared in
the *Kansas City Times*.

Library of Congress Cataloging-in-Publication Data
Fulghum, Robert.
All I really need to know I learned in kindergarten:
the essay that became a classic/by Robert Fulghum.
p.   cm.
"With a special commentary by Robert Fulghum."
ISBN 0-394-58894-0
1. Life. I. Title.
BD431.F84   1990   128—dc20   90-42252

Manufactured in the United States of America
5 7 9 8 6 4

Book design and calligraphy by Carole Lowenstein

For all who love learning enough to teach

OST OF US are partners in a powerful publishing company. An underground press of sorts, dealing in reprints of cartoons, pithy sayings, poems, short declarations, and those pictures worth a thousand words.

If you are one of those who look for such things and often reproduce them on the office copy machine to stick on bulletin boards where you work and on the refrigerator at home, then you are part of the People's Publishing Company.

Nobody pays you to do this.

You do it simply because an item has moved your mind—made you think or cry or laugh enough to want to pass it on to someone else.

It goes on the refrigerator because you want to see it again. You want it out there in plain sight because it is very important.

Any author whose work is selected for the Refrigerator Award should feel highly honored. Not even winning the Nobel Prize will get a writer's words into the kitchen of everyday life and up on the fridge.

Some time in 1985, a short essay most people call "That Thing About Kindergarten" won the International Refrigerator Award. It also won the Office Bulletin Board Sweepstakes, the Send-a-Copy-to-Your-Mom Trophy, and the Neighborhood-Newsletter Silver Cup. Even the My-Rabbi-Read-It-in-His-Sermon Prize.

Like Jack in the story about the beanstalk, "Kindergarten" went out into the world on its own and had some amazing adventures. As I write now, in the spring of 1990, "That Thing About Kindergarten" has traveled around the globe—translated into at least nineteen languages (all the major ones you might expect, but in Korean, Finnish, Turkish, Slovene, Magyar, and Hebrew as well).

And it became the title essay of the book, *All I Really Need to Know I Learned in Kindergarten,* which has sold several million copies in at least seventy-three countries.

The essay hangs in the halls of the U.S. Congress, on the walls of schools, and in prison cells. You can find it in high-tech scientific laboratories, your doctor's waiting room, and factory cafeterias. Once it turned up in the telephone bills of the six million customers of Southwestern Bell. Travelers report seeing it in China, Russia, and South Africa. And if that is not enough, "That Thing About Kindergarten" was stitched into a sampler by a high-school student for a 4-H project, and it took the first prize at the Iowa State Fair.

The author of the kindergarten essay had his life turned topsy-turvy by it.

I know.

I am he.

Recently, to get some perspective on this whole hoo-ha in preparation for writing this introduction, I stuck a copy of "Kindergarten" to the door of my own refrigerator (with four industrial magnets—none of those little cute ceramic deals for me—when

I stick something on the fridge, it stays stuck). Anyhow . . . I sat in my kitchen one night and stared at the lines that had altered my life and wondered: Why?

Why these words? Why me?

And most of all I wondered: Is it REALLY true that all I really need to know I learned in kindergarten?

On a quick critical read, the essay might easily be dismissed as greeting-card-level fluff. A bit simple-minded, naïve, cute, intellectually superficial.

The essay breaks the standard rule that important things are supposed to be hard to understand.

On the other hand, the essay answers the question asked sooner or later by every schoolchild staring out the window from a classroom desk and wondering: "Why am I here? Why do I have to go to school?"

We are sent to school to be civilized.

To be initiated into the most profound mysteries of society.

We are sent out of the home to meet the truth of the world.

Almost always, the "world" turns out to be school. And no matter what that place of beginning in the world is called—day-care, kindergarten, first grade—the experience is the same.

From the first day we are told in language we can understand what has come to be prized as the foundation of community and culture. The teacher calls these first lessons "simple rules," but they are in fact the distillation of all the hard-won, field-tested fundamentals of civilization itself.

Not only are we told about these things, but we soon discover that we are in a lab course—we are going to be asked to live these precepts every day.

And they are not, it turns out, simple after all. No. *Elemental* is the word.

A carbon atom may be simply expressed in the symbol C, atomic number 6, but it is essential to the structure of life itself. Elemental. Not simple—with extremely complex implications.

I repeat. We are sent to school to be civilized.

And it is a bedrock value of civilization that knowledge is better than ignorance. We have found out the hard way. Experience and wisdom gained in the great march of humankind must be shared and passed on if the march is to continue.

What we learn in kindergarten will come up again and again in our lives as long as we live. In far more complex, polysyllabic forms, to be sure—lectures, encyclopedias, bibles, company rules, courts of law,

sermons, and handbooks. We will be tested and examined over the years to see if we understand what
we have learned.

Across the course of our lives we will wrestle with
questions of right and wrong, good and bad, truth
and lies. Again and again and yet again, we will come
around to the place where we came in—to that room
where the elemental notions about the human enter-
prise were handed to us with great care when we
were very young—in kindergarten.

FULGHUM

Each spring, for many years,
I have set myself the task of writing
a personal statement of belief: a Credo.
When I was younger, the statement ran
for many pages, trying to cover every base,
with no loose ends. It sounded like
a Supreme Court brief, as if words
could resolve all conflicts about
the meaning of existence.

The Credo has grown shorter in recent years—
sometimes cynical, sometimes comical,
sometimes bland — but I keep working at it.
Recently I set out to get the
statement of personal belief down to one page
in simple terms, fully understanding the
naïve idealism that implied.

The inspiration for brevity came to me at a gasoline station. I managed to fill an old car's tank with super-deluxe high-octane go-juice. My old hoopy couldn't handle it and got the willies — kept sputtering out at intersections and belching going downhill.

I understood.

My mind and my spirit get like that
from time to time. Too much high-content
information and <u>I</u> get the existential willies—
keep sputtering out at intersections
where life choices must be made
and I either know too much or not enough.
The examined life is no picnic.

I realized then that I already know
most of what's necessary to live a meaningful life—
that it isn't all that complicated.
I know it.
And have known it for a long, long time.
Living it—well, that's another matter, yes?
Here's my Credo:

ALL I REALLY NEED TO KNOW
about how to live and what to do and
how to be I learned in kindergarten.
Wisdom was not at the top of
the graduate-school mountain, but
there in the sandpile at Sunday School.
These are the things I learned:

Share
everything.

· 23 ·

Play fair.

Don't
hit people.

Put things back
where you
found them.

· 26 ·

Clean up
your own mess.

Don't take things that aren't yours.

Say you're sorry
when you
hurt somebody.

Wash your hands
before you eat.

Warm cookies
and cold milk
are good for you.

· 32 ·

Live a balanced life—
learn some and
think some and
draw and paint and
sing and dance and
play and work
every day some.

Take a nap
every
afternoon.

· 34 ·

When you go out
into the world,
watch out for traffic,
hold hands, and
stick together.

Be aware of wonder.
Remember the little seed
in the Styrofoam cup:
The roots go down and
the plant goes up and nobody
really knows how or why,
but we are all like that.
Goldfish and hamsters
and white mice and even
the little seed in the
Styrofoam cup—they all die.
So do we.

And then remember the
Dick-and-Jane books
and the first word
you learned—the biggest
word of all—

LOOK.

Everything you need to know
is in there somewhere.
The Golden Rule and love and
basic sanitation.
Ecology and politics and equality
and sane living.
Take any one of those items and
extrapolate it into sophisticated adult terms
and apply it to your family life or
your work or your government or
your world and it holds true
and clear and firm.

· 38 ·

Think what a better world it would be
if we all — the whole world—had
cookies and milk about three o'clock
every afternoon and then lay down
with our blankies for a nap.
Or if all governments had as a basic policy
to always put things back where
they found them and to clean up
their own mess.

And it is still true,
no matter how old you are—
when you go out into the world,
it is best to hold hands and
stick together.

ABOUT THE AUTHOR

ROBERT FULGHUM is the author of
All I Really Need to Know I Learned in Kindergarten
and *It Was on Fire When I Lay Down on It.*